SELECTED POEMS

LESLIE NORRIS
SELECTED POEMS

United States distributor
DUFOUR EDITIONS, INC.
Chester Springs, PA 19425
Tel. (215) 458-5005

POETRY WALES PRESS
1986

POETRY WALES PRESS
56 PARCAU AVENUE, BRIDGEND, MID GLAMORGAN

British Library Cataloguing in Publication Data

Norris, Leslie
    Selected poems.
    I. Title
    821'.914   PR6027.044

ISBN 0-907476-60-0

The publisher acknowledges the financial support of the
Welsh Arts Council

Cover Painting: The Merthyr to Brecon Road by Alan Salisbury
Cover design by Jeane Rees

Typeset by Wordsmiths Ltd.
Printed in 10 point Plantin
by Antony Rowe Ltd., Chippenham.

CONTENTS

from RANSOMS

from MOUNTAINS POLECATS PHEASANTS

from *WATER VOICES*

NEW POEMS

These poems were first published in:

The Loud Winter (Triskel Press, 1967)
Finding Gold (The Hogarth Press, 1967)
Ransoms (Chatto & Windus, 1971)
Mountains Polecats Pheasants (Chatto & Windus, 1974)
Water Voices (Chatto & Windus, 1980)

from *THE LOUD WINTER*

Autumn Elegy

September. The small summer hangs its suns
On the chestnuts, and the world bends slowly
Out of the year. On tiles of the low barns
The lingering swallows rest in this timely

Warmth, collecting it. Standing in the garden,
I too feel its generosity; but would not leave.
Time, time to lock the heart. Nothing is sudden
In Autumn, yet the long, ceremonial passion of

The year's death comes quickly enough
As firm veins shut on the sluggish blood
And the numberless protestations of the leaf
Are mapped on the air. Live wood

Was scarce and bony where I lived as a boy.
I am not accustomed to such opulent
Panoply of dying. Yet, if I stare
Unmoved at the flaunting, silent

Agony in the country before a resonant
Wind anneals it, I am not diminished, it is not
That I do not see well, do not exult,
But that I remember again what

Young men of my own time died
In the Spring of their living and could not turn
To this. They died in their flames, hard
War destroyed them. Now as the trees burn

In the beginning glory of Autumn
I sing for all green deaths as I remember
In their broken Mays, and turn
The years back for them, every red September.

The Old Age of Llywarch Hen

My crutch, see, Autumn is with us;
The fern burns red and harvest is in the house.
I have put away my strength and my promise.

I see in the evening the fire-smoke climb
And the earlier dusk send the children home
To their cool beds, their milk, their mothers' warm

Love in the hospitable house of youth
Where once I too had room and all the truth
I wanted was in four small walls. Now death

Examines everything I do. I need
A crutch, an abominable leg of wood
To hold me upright. I have a cold heart and a savage head.

Crutch there, do you hear the loud winter?
Young men go to the inn, singing as they enter,
But here in my room is the world's lonely centre

Where the voices of the young are the voices
Of ghosts. I know no young faces.
None come to see me. The young have their own places

In light and warmth and love. Which I knew
When my legs could carry me for two
Hill days and my breath was a long Halloo!

O my crutch, when spring was alive!
When loud were the undoing birds, like a dove
The smooth air. And girls offered their love

In all the bright Mays that a race of days
Chased past! Of all coloured plays
I remember these best. Old days, dead days.

Crutch, what if I burn you? Shall my age
Wither in the destroying flame, will my drudge
Body renew? It is a hopeless dream. I must trudge

Three-legged whatever ways are left, though rain
Renew the receptive fields. Stumbling and winter pain
Are what I know best. I'll not see Spring again.

Early Frost

We were warned about frost, yet all day the summer
Has wavered its heat above the empty stubble. Late
Bees hung their blunt weight,
Plump drops between those simplest wings, their leisure
An ignorance of frost.
My mind is full of the images of summer
And a liquid curlew calls from alps of air;

But the frost has come. Already under trees
Pockets of summer are dying, wide paths
Of the cold glow clean through the stricken thickets
And again I feel on my cheek the cut of winters
Dead. Once I awoke in a dark beyond moths
To a world still with freezing,
Hearing my father go to the yard for his ponies,

His hands full of frostnails to point their sliding
To a safe haul. I went to school,
Socks pulled over shoes for the streets' clear glass,
The early shops cautious, the tall
Classroom windows engraved by winter's chisel,
Fern, feather and flower that would not let the pale
Day through. We wrote in a cold fever for the morning

Play. Then boys in the exulting yard, ringing
Boots hard on winter, slapped with their polishing
Caps the arrows of their gliding, in steaming lines
Ran till they launched one by one
On the skills of ice their frail balance,
Sliding through time with not a fall in mind,
Their voices crying freely through such shouting

As the cold divided I slid in the depth
Of the season till the swung bell sang us in.
Now insidious frost, its parched grains rubbing
At crannies, moved on our skin.
Our fingers died. Not the warmth
Of all my eight wide summers could keep me smiling.
The circle of the popping stove fell still

And we were early sped through the hurrying dark.
I ran through the bitterness on legs
That might have been brittle, my breath
Solid, grasping at stabs of bleak
Pain to gasp on. Winter branched in me, ice cracked
In my bleeding. When I fell through the teeth
Of the cold at my haven door I could not see

For locked tears, I could not feel the spent
Plenty of flames banked at the range,
Nor my father's hands as they roughed the blue
Of my knees. But I knew what he meant
With the love of his rueful laugh, and my true
World unfroze in a flood of happy crying,
As hot on my cheek as the sting of this present

Frost. I have stood too long in the orderly
Cold of the garden, I would not have again the death
Of that day come unasked as the comfortless dusk
Past the stakes of my fences. Yet these are my
Ghosts, they do not need to ask
For housing when the early frost comes down.
I take them in, all, to the settled warmth.

Snow

The snow surprised us, coming
   When it did,
A sudden white swarm, humming
   Out of the long cloud.
Winter, with a cold deciduous voice,
Came briskly and purposefully upon us,

And our secure horizon
   Retracted
To a warm room's bounds. But children
   Swanked into the yard,
Their warm laughter twirling the prodigal snow
Into peaks, columns, ghosts – the afternoon glow

Was evergreen memory for them.
   So we all,
Warmed, went to the window, away from
   The surly fire. The tall
Snow fell, and thicket, hedge and fence,
Familiar limits all, burned so with snow's radiance

As to delight, renew us.
   And we saw,
Thirty years clearer our eyes,
   Ourselves, puffed round with scarves,
Like rainbow robins bounce on the stiff-legged snow,
Innocently singing with voices lost long ago.

An Old House

Seeing him near the wall, I call my dog.
He lifts his head and its unholy eye.
An old dog knows the form and will not fall.
He moves towards me with a tolerant sigh,

An amiable dog. He shines against the light
His vigorous coat, and sits. Together we
Approach with care the fall I called him from,
Stop, and stare down. The river flushes by

Its melancholy brown. Old weeds, round stones
Are covered with its rusts down to the bend
Where, noisy as its cans, it disappears.
A bankrupt factory now holds the land

The old house owned, the house in which we played.
Rising in spasms from the ruined stairs,
The chastened sun was lost in puffs of dust
And the wild rooms moved coldly through their tears.

Caught in our play, we searched for that sad mark
The meek stabbed girl had at her murder made,
Running from sunlight into the vigilant dark.
That I was slow was not I was afraid,

But I did not believe. I heard my friends above
Run laughing through the green and peeling places,
In fungus rioting, in dry rot. The spent wood
Hung cobwebs from soft rafters in their faces.

And while I said I did, I could not see
How any struck girl in her ropes of blood
Could drive her thumb, soft palm, indelible whorl,
Inch deep into the stone before she died.

So when the voices stopped there came for me
A static moment out of time's command;
In that brief sky the impermanent birds still fly,
That mummied summer, still its airs suspend

In dead perfection, and ghosts put on their flesh.
For these are ghosts, the boys who from this house
Burst with hysteria in their spitting feet,
The whimpering ends of laughter in their mouths:

Then life caught up its breath, and I ran with them,
What they had seen I could not make them say.
In the harsh sun I found my freckled courage,
Jeered, was angry, went home a different way.

And walk a different way for a whole life.
Five simple years soon took them to the war
That burned their vision on all Europe's houses.
In the old house it was their death they saw.

After such roads I stand in the rind of the day
With my poor ghosts. Headlights stain the snow,
Light leaves the monotonous sky. Heavy with night,
Down the steep hill the wary motorists go,

Stiff on the packed ice. I whistle to my dog;
His eyes rejoice. The fall I call him from.
Now winter bellows through the travellers' air
And with a sigh I tell the dead go home.

The Ballad of Billy Rose

Outside Bristol Rovers Football Ground –
The date has gone from me, but not the day,
Nor how the dissenting flags in stiff array
Struck bravely out against the sky's grey round –

Near the Car Park then, past Austin and Ford,
Lagonda, Bentley, and a colourful patch
Of country coaches come in for the match
Was where I walked, having travelled the road

From Fishponds to watch Portsmouth in the Cup.
The Third Round, I believe. And I was filled
With the old excitement which had thrilled
Me so completely when, while growing up,

I went on Saturdays to match or fight.
Not only me; for thousands of us there
Strode forward eagerly, each man aware
Of tingling memory, anticipating delight.

We all marched forward, all except one man.
I saw him because he was paradoxically still,
A stone against the flood, face upright against us all,
Head bare, hoarse voice aloft, blind as a stone.

I knew him at once, despite his pathetic clothes;
Something in his stance, or his sturdy frame
Perhaps, I could even remember his name
Before I saw it on his blind-man's tray. Billy Rose.

And twenty forgetful years fell away at the sight.
Bare-kneed, dismayed, memory fled to the hub
Of Saturday violence, with friends to the Labour Club,
Watching the boxing on a sawdust summer night.

The boys' enclosure close to the shabby ring
Was where we stood, clenched in a resin world,
Spoke in cool voices, lounged, were artificially bored
During minor bouts. We paid threepence to go in.

Billy Rose fought there. He was top of the bill.
So brisk a fighter, so gallant, so precise!
Trim as a tree he stood for the ceremonies,
Then turned to meet George Morgan of Tirphil.

He had no chance. Courage was not enough,
Nor tight defence. Donald Davies was sick
And we threatened his cowardice with an embarrassed kick.
Ripped across both his eyes was Rose, but we were tough

And clapped him as they wrapped his blindness up
In busy towels, applauded the wave
He gave his executioners, cheered the brave
Blind man as he cleared with a jaunty hop

The top rope. I had forgotten that day
As if it were dead for ever, yet now I saw
The flowers of punched blood on the ring floor,
As bright as his name, I do not know

How long I stood with ghosts of the wild fists
And the cries of shaken boys long dead around me,
For struck to act at last, in terror and pity
I threw some frantic money, three treacherous pence –

And I cry at the memory – into his tray, and ran,
Entering the waves of the stadium like a drowning man.
Poor Billy Rose. God, he could fight
Before my three sharp coins knocked out his sight.

Picking Coal

I had thought until this late wind shook the wall
Winter had ended, but doors have banged all night
In the grumbling house,
Telling the sleepless about the entering weather.
A malignant cold, unwelcome, it turns the heart.

I remember a day like this, out of place in the warm
Young year. Frail sun licked the killed buds,
Ferns hung in the stopped
Threads of their fronds. Our breathing unseasonably
Flowered, we were walking the weather away.

Weather is all summer for boys in their confidence,
The sun inhabits them, their touch replenishes
What spoiled branches
They choose in their lucky vigour. But the land
So grown from our morning wishes, a blossoming country,

Was struck by abrupt black winter in a killing pyramid.
Our eyes could not fructify this. Death of the earth
Came in high cradles
From a harsh, close mine, on laborious wires,
Clumsily, inevitably. The dry axles' melancholy

Scraping squealed in the air like a disease of birds
And the heaped slag dropped, load on load,
Bones of the ripped pit's
Waste. Perched sliding, a man with his weak
Pick scratched among rattling for small knobs

Of lost coal, to warm in his sack. His long
Rags dragged in the dirt. He lived with winter.
Of his voice as he spoke
Across years and seasons through the cloud of his labour
I do not know, nor tell of his thin, pale wrist

That no rubbed grime could strengthen. His decay grew
From the burned spoil where he stood. We were circled
By impregnable light and sun
And could not understand him, nor his sudden anger.
We offered him a cigarette from a rich packet,

But he refused, turning away with useless dignity.
It was golden David, so soon to die in exploding Europe,
Who lit up and smoked.
Now in my indolent, midsummer forties, hammocked in
     comfort,
It is this coldest wind disturbs, turning the heart.

from FINDING GOLD

More than Half Way There

Obsessed by night, my young voice told
Of swallows' ruby eyes between such trees
As the cool moon allowed, and their dark
Flight, elaborately simple, their desire
Unthinkingly perfect, and their perfect songs.

That was long ago. I use my nights for twitching
Sleep now, and what stern birds parade
In the iron trees do not disturb me.
I walk in the afternoons. The common
Blackbird sings and I accept this marvel.

To protect any true voice, even one like this,
Means constant vigilance. Each day I watch
An older hand take the food to my mouth.
I am alert lest an old voice soften
What needs to be said. Guard. Silence if necessary.

Dead Boys

Here is the field, beneath two hundred houses,
Where the boy
Buried a dead bird.
He felt for it a small, universal sadness,
And gave it a birthday sixpence, all he had.
Among these urban gardens his remembered tears
Are old now, and real as the unravelling breezes
That thirty years blew all his griefs to dry.

The pond was here, its arid grains are laid
Higher than boys
About these flimsy garages.
All night long, all one long winter night,
The old tin Fords stood with their headlights turned
On its drowning ice, thin as a ripped sheet,
Where the covered slider lay in his silent bubbles
And would not be found. His school cap wrongly floated.

His name was known. The women sailed it
On gentle breath
Where they stood by the
Powerless cars in a darkness beyond rescue.
Gliding alone in the cold of a frozen death
He had not realised, the boy in his eyeless sight
Saw the face of the drowned, and held it
For simple mourning. He heard the desperate

Cursing of helpless fathers as weak ice kept
Them impotent.
Days are long to a boy;
Nights buried his foundered sadness in their tides
Till the black hulks slept in softness, as he slept.
Once he was thoughtless to an easy friend. The roads
Of summer led them away and they broke in a rough
     moment,
Never to meet again. It was here that he said goodbye

To his angular childhood. He walks the streets,
Their garish doors
Open to the field long gone,
And the grown man smiles as returning he meets,
In his eyed love, the cold, immortal children.
They run unblighted the green lanes of their time,
They laugh, their bright innocence unknown around them;
Here, where the field was, they live, the dead boys.

An Evening by the Lake

Well, let us admit it, I make
A pleasant picture here. A check
Overcoat, fresh from the cleaners,
Discreet suede shoes (I use a wire brush),
Trouser-legs, that new bronze-green colour,
Just narrow enough for good taste.
I walk briskly, waving now and then and
Gently, a tweed hat.
Even my dog, unfashionable but
Successful, adds to my satisfaction.
She is obedient, but not servile.
On this grey evening, here at the edge
Of the lake and under the clouds,
She skips on the washed grass and is
Complacently white.
                  I have not lived
In the town for twenty years.

But walked this lakeside drive four times
A day when a boy, going to school
In a comic Gothic castle, built
For a fat iron-master. It turns
A stolid, limestone gaze down at
Me now.
           The park is quite deserted,
But for some poor boys, younger
Than I was, playing a thoughtless
Game a long way off. I watch them
Lift a great dressed stone, from
An old wall perhaps, stagger the few
Uneven yards to the water,
Then drop the huge thing in. I see
The little fountain of its drowning,
Then the slow circles spread. Boys' voices
Bounce to me over the resilient water.

Later I hear the stone's loud splash,
Much later.
                    Four of us on this lake,
Using two boats, once rowed for the price
Of their hire a furious race. Off
To a gasped start, we plunged our oars
For all our thin arms' worth,
Driving the clumsy prows through
Burst reflections of the full clouds
And green banks. When I lifted my
Dripping blade from the water, (Dan
Chanting our time), I could see behind
The lovely dimpling of its leaving
The liquid skin.
                    Then at last we stopped,
And called, our high voices skidding
Like flat, thrown stones over the resonant
Surface.
                    Just like these later voices,
And this younger water, which have
Entered the locked cellar of my mind,
Broken its seal, and let its darkness
Out.
        So that I stand alone and
Bowed, on a scuffed, gravel path, in
A shabby park, my legs tired, my
Heart shaken, my jaunty clothes all
Wrong. All right, so my youth is dead.
And yes, those boys are gone.

A February Morning

This February morning, walking early to work
Across the frost-hung fields where the mild cattle
Stand wreathed in their own breath, I watch smooth
Starlings, loud handfuls of shot silk,
And hear my steps echo on the iron rime of the time.

Just as they echoed so sharply time out of mind ago
In my own country's cold
On the Dowlais moors at the dark of night
With one fierce unnatural star
Alone in the sky's arch.
Along the uncertain edge of the hanging mountain
The wild ponies limped and trembled,
Ice chiming like bells
In the long hair of their flanks. My footsteps,
Picked clean out of the cold and country air,
Hung their thin images on the ear's sharpness
For miles along the road
With never a near light nor comfortable sound.

But gently, and from no apparent direction,
The voice of a singing woman used the air,
Unhurried, passionate, clear, a voice of grief
Made quite impersonal by the night and hour.
For full five minutes' space along that mountain,
Not loudly nor ever fading away,
A full voice sang
Of such inhuman longing that I no more
Can say which was the song or which the fiery star.
One or the other lit the hollow road
That lay behind my clipped and winter steps
Time out of mind ago, in Wales.

This frosty morning, across the February fields
The militant bush of the sun in tawny splendour
Has not extinguished it, that song or star.

The Quarrel

Unable to sleep I turn from the comfortless bed
And watch where the night turns all our roofs to metal;
The world's inhuman now and has its consequent peace.
I see you sadly asleep on the grateful sheets
That are for me ropes, knouts, hard instruments;
I am glad of these circumstances. It is not long
Since my deliberate savagery made you desperate
And you waited too long for any contrition at all.

When I pretend that the best words come in the dark
And you are asleep as I speak them to the deaf moon,
For such dishonesty the night rejects my fever
And the malevolent furniture sneers from its corners.

Rain

Rain, bleak rain, is enough to set aside
The positive comfort of my solid roof;
Its harsh brush scrubs aside all
That I cannot see, the housed world
Is open to rain. I recognise
Its crepitations on my skin, its pocks
Slap hard on my neck. Gently, with
Unrelieved alarm, I feel my unwet
Flesh. I lie in the narrow
Warmth of the bed, hoping for the first
Tentative cry of the day-stirred
Blackbird, for the small thunder of the flying
Pigeons to carry the night away.

The Strong Man

On my way to school I saw the man,
His little audience on the Square
Brought me abruptly running there.
Few on that boyhood afternoon
Had interest enough to spare,
Or money, to watch a rough tramp bare

To the waist perform his common tricks.
Incurious time had begun to wear
Haphazard patterns on his skin, to blur
The heavy flesh. He tore his packs
Of seedy cards, snapped through the air
The chains we'd thought as strong as care,

Leaving them empty on the ground.
Then, with a kind of wry despair,
He took a yard of iron bar,
Raised it, and brought it breaking down
On his own forearm. And over,
And over, boots kicking the floor,

The brisk tips sparking, until it had
Bent round his arm. His furious tonsure
Stung with sweat, his lips puffed lather,
The great ribs rasped. He stooped to the road
For his traps, his ripped shirt. We
Cheered his freedom: if such are free.

Rome Remembered

Wet on the slate roofs and the yard awash;
No football for the day. I looked from my desk
At two cold boys lost on the Welsh tips,
Their hands fumbling, their frail knees
Scarred as mine from too many a
Reckless fall, the drill rain
Needling incessantly their dark pelts,
Their round, dark heads.

From what deep mouth of their need
The she-wolf came I do not remember.
The ripped sack of her coat,
Her narrow legs, her cautious feet asprawl,
There she was
In all the loud smell of her dampness.
She covered her foul teeth, her brute head bowed.
The wolf is a poor creature at best.

But they recognised her animal rescue,
Her warm dugs grey as coal, and lived.
They turned from a whimpering den to build
On any seven of our hills a mythical city.
Rome stands in the raw towers
Of fallen steelworks, her eagle
Sails on the walls of sacked blast-furnaces,
Cinders cover her emperors.
Broken Remus is dead on the high moors.

A Sense of History

Walking at random over the mountainous moorland
With cry of curlew and wild mare's warning neigh
Held in an unhedged wind enough to knock your head off,
At the bitter end of a swept and solitary day

I came at last to the shores of an incongruous water
Perched without purpose upon a mountain summit.
The eastern end was a shelving bank of stone
And the terrible wind blew stiff waves upon it.

And, head down along the edge, I could not help notice
How all the long perimeter was similarly guarded
With single slices of stone, each patiently placed
Against the waves' water and into a crude mosaic.

Who dry-walled these shores? What men had planned
These back-breaking banks and lived on the low
Secure island? (It is there still, and still the stone
Ungainly circles that were houses how long ago).

I only know that I was suddenly kneeling –
While over me flew the torn, unheeding froth –
And plugging with scales of stone the wave-worn gaps,
Ten frozen fingers against the loud storm's tooth.

Then heading homeward through the embracing marshland,
I faithfully found with quick and unearned skill
The hidden paths that led to the acquired valley,
Quite dry and hidden, away from wind, lake, hill.

Man and Boy

I and the white-faced boy I have to comfort
Walk in the lemon sunlight after our shadows,
He rocked with sobs and I talking kindly of nothing.

The afternoon train hurls its weight beyond the two meadows,
Leaving behind it a silence unbearably sad
Where the child is aloof and alone in his oval of grief,

His body bent, and his desolate landscape in tears.
For me the butterflies dance – and I hope he will see them –
Over the gardens where boys grow improbable flowers;

But winter's his world and something has broken his laughter.
So I keep him with me and we walk from the school to
    the gardens,
I walking alone, and he quite alone in his sorrow.

Soon he will stop and let the brave sunlight take over
The whole of his eyes, and flowers and butterflies prancing
Make up a new minute for generous summer to enter.

But I shall be left insidiously moved and troubled
As he runs through the playground kicking a stone before
    him,
Aware of my young despair and remembered terror.

He will cry in his sleep tonight, his small body turning
Through arcs of sadness that carry him out of his darkness:
I shall not cure his wounds, though my own scars are burning.

Gardening Gloves

Mild, knob-jointed, old,
They lie on the garage floor.
Scarred by the turn of a spade
In hard, agricultural wear
And soiled by seasonal mould
They *look* like animal skins –
Or imagine a gargoyle's hands.

But not my hands I'd swear,
Being large, rough and uncouth;
Yet the moment I pick them up
They assume an absurd truth,
They assert I have given them shape,
Making my hands the mirror
For their comfortable horror.

And I know if I put them on
I gain a deliberate skill,
An old, slow satisfaction
That is not mine at all
But sent down from other men.
Yes, dead men live again
In my reluctant skin.

I remember my father's hands,
How they moved as mine do now
While he took his jokes from the air
Like precise, comical birds.
These gloves are my proper wear.
We all preserve such lives.
I'm not sorry to have these gloves.

Looking at Snowdrops

Bursts through the rusty hedge the torn wind,
Turns, and with its last flap lifts
From their bent holds the ruffled finches,
Then softly drops them back
On other perches, bobbing, bobbing.

We walk past a cold bridge
In whose hard spars
A stiff girl clings that she may catch
Water's seductive shadows in
Her sharp viewfinder. A paperback
Hart Crane bumps in my jacket pocket
As I stump, chill, along.

When we see them, two fields away, great sheets
Of the small white snowdrops, my love,
Her eyes blazed by such urgent purity,
Exclaims them for water, sees them
Wide pools in the low grass, with small white waves
Genuinely gathered by the afternoon's cutting

Air. Now we step off the thin path
Among lakes of the flowers.
And this is disturbing. So might
That sauntering, sad Hart Crane, his
Solid boat set far homeward in the seapaths,
Have walked off into the waves,
Stepped no less easily into the deep sea,
$$\text{bobbing, bobbing,}$$

Was drowned, yes, he was drowned.
In acres of white froth
And an orchard of rocks.

Buzzard

With infinitely confident little variations of his finger-ends
He soothes the erratic winds.
He hangs on air's gap, then turns
On royal wing into his untouchable circle.
All, all, lie under his sifting eye,
The squat man, the sheep, the mouse in the slate cleft.

He is not without pity for he does not know pity.
He is a machine for killing; searchlight eye,
Immaculate wing, then talon and hook.
He kills without cruelty for he does not know cruelty.

If he fails in a small death he is awkward. And angry,
Loosing upon the hills his terrible, petulant cry.
To fail often is to die.
His livelihood is such single-minded and obsessional artistry.

He is not seduced by emotion
Or impeccable clear thought even
Into considerations other than his pure life.

We observe our prey doubtfully,
Behind many hedges and in tufted country.
Even when we see it clear
Have too many words to kill it.

Curlew

Dropped from the air at evening, this desolate call
Mocks us, who listen to its delicate non-humanity.
Dogs smile, cats flatter, cows regard us all
With eyes like those of ladies in a city,

So that we transfer to them familiar human virtues
To comfort and keep us safe. But this adamant bird
With the plaintive throat and curved, uneasy jaws
Crying creates a desert with a word

More terrible than chaos, and we stand at the edge
Of nothing. How shall we know its purpose, this wild
      bird,
Whose world is not confined by the linnets' hedge,
Whose mouth lets fly the appalling cry we heard?

The Old Year

Winter appoints its frosts, and the hedges blaze
With as many cold flames as light the tideless dark.
Ice holds the crackling ruts. I am reluctant
To leave the warm house, fooling that a soft book
Uses me seriously. Yet I should stand
Under a deep tree in a field of frost fire,
Hearing the call of owls, watching the rough old year
Gustily fronting its death with a brutal wind.

Aware of Death

At two-thirty in the morning I awoke choking,
Every fibre in my fur-lined lungs roaring
For relief of air, the room unhinged and bellowing
And the crazy window swimming in and out
Of two dabbed eyes. Take it easy, take it easy,
Said my unseated reason. Or feeble courage, I don't know
Like hell, I thought, like hell I'll take it easy.
I began to nurse the oxygen like a miser,
Controlled the rasping walls with a shrewd squint,
Tucked rasping panic into an obscure corner,
And found I was easier. My arms for example.
I had thought them wildly pummelling the night for breath,
But they were confident on two clasped fists of sheet,
Calmly supporting my racked and labouring body.
I pulled carefully with my mouth at the painful
Air. It was like drinking straight out of a cold tap.

And nothing like this had ever happened to me before.

Later I lay for twenty minutes by the cold moon
In a metal sweat of fever, yes, but as well of
Almost the final terror, my lungs boiling,
Tongue too big for talk, mouth
Tasting the body's bitter dissolution;
Aware of death.

Nightingales

I

My namesake, old Bill Norris, standing beneath a tree
So bitterly gnarled he might have grown from it, stopped
Talking to listen, lifted eyes dayblue and delighted,
And laughed a silent pleasure. "There's a good many,"
He said, "Walks past as close as you and never hears her,
Though she sings as bright in the hot noon as any night."
Two feet above his head the dun bird pulsed and lilted.
It was in this village and perhaps for this same bird
I lay awake the whole of one miraculous darkness.
She sang so close to my house I could have touched
Her singing; I could not breathe through the aching silences.
And for nights after, hunched among pillows, I grabbed
At any sleep at all, hearing the nightingale
Hammer my plaintive rest with remorseless melody.
Full of resented ecstasy, I groaned nightlong in my bed.

II

Or driving one Sunday morning in Maytime Hampshire
On our way to a christening in one of the villages,
We stopped on Steep Hill, the road climbing headily upwards.
In the first warm air of the year we looked down on the
Trees, unmoving and full in the freshness of their leaves.
There were eight nightingales, eight, they filled the valley
With sobbing, the cataracts of their voices fell
Erratically among the splendid beeches. Open-eyed
We stood on the lip of the hill, while near and far
The water-notes of their singing grew faint, were lost almost,
Answered and redoubled near at hand, trailed
Dropping sadly down the valley-sides, struck purely out
With sound round notes into the listening morning.

We were still with music, as the day was. That we were
    late
For the christening was to the credit of those nightingales.

III

When I was very young my father took me from bed,
Dressed me in haste, and we walked into the night.
Winter was so long gone I had forgotten darkness.
We went by paths which in daylight knew me well,
But now were strange with shadow. It was not long
Before we came to the wood where the nightingale sang,
The unbelievable bird who lived in the stories
Of almost my every book. Would it sing, would it sing?
I thought the wood was full of silent listeners.
I do not remember it singing. My father carried me home,
My head rolling back on its stalk at every measure
Of his deep stride, and all I have brought back
From that long night are the fixed stars reeling.
It is the poet's bird, they say. Perhaps I took it home,
For here I am, raising my voice, scraping my throat raw again.

Finding Gold

From his house each day the child moves to school
Through a deliberate ceremony. He is obsessed
By a chosen maze, marking his ritual
With clear jumps over long stones full
Of inescapable bad luck, then a stick's rattle
Briskly along twenty-three exact bars of tall
Fence outside the bus station; the road crossed
Here, always. His frail, unswerving rule
Is to impose order on a chaotic world.

Pressed by his abiding route, he mounts the stone
Parapet. One step to the edge and, elate
With danger, coldly he stares down at
The diminished water. Freckled mallows fret
At the shallow runs. Slowly, slowly now, must
He turn and saunter with rehearsed arrogance the lane
Through the sagging garages, slack doors on the yawn.
He will not move his head when shadows threaten,
Nor falter a slid inch from his restricted cobbles.

But here in a sunny gap between two sheds
Is a circle of stone seats, loosely deserted.
Black as police stand the rough walls, the gamblers
Are running down tittering alleys, their cards
Scattered as windfalls, their copper bets
Spilled in fallen coils. The quick child
Hurries deep coins into the crannies of his pockets
And breaks for school. All safe custom run wild,
He laughs in the tumble of the anonymous playground.

All day he sat in school, full of pennies
To his round eyes. He thought without moving
Of springing circles of stone standing inches
Outside his orderly magic, and knew for us

All, one step from broken practice the spread gold lies,
In the green lanes of absence. Are his coins living?
Does he stride on the mapless hills where the gamblers'
Dust is lifted? Is he stumping his trodden roads
With an old day turning, stupidly turning?

from RANSOMS

Cardigan Bay

for Kitty

The buzzard hung crossed
On the air and we came
Down from the hills under
Him. First sun from
The underworld turned
White his stretched surfaces,
Whitened the cracked stone

On this beach where end
The works of the sea,
The total husbandry
Of water. Now at noon
We walk the land between
The seamarks, knowing

That wave already made
To wash away our happy
Loitering before
We turn back into evening
Among the frail daffodils
Growing in other seasons.

For those who live here
After our daylight, I
Could wish us to look
Out of the darkness
We have become, teaching
Them happiness, a true love.

Water

On hot summer mornings my aunt set glasses
On a low wall outside the farmhouse,
With some jugs of cold water.
I would sit in the dark hall, or
      Behind the dairy window,
Waiting for children to come from the town.

They came in small groups, serious, steady,
And I could see them, black in the heat,
Long before they turned in at our gate
To march up the soft, dirt road.
      They would stand by the wall,
Drinking water with an engrossed thirst. The dog

Did not bother them, knowing them responsible
Travellers. They held in quiet hands their bags
Of jam sandwiches, and bottles of yellow fizz.
Sometimes they waved a gratitude to the house,
      But they never looked at us.
Their eyes were full of the mountain, lifting

Their measuring faces above our long hedge.
When they had gone I would climb the wall,
Looking for them among the thin sheep runs.
Their heads were a resolute darkness among ferns,
      They climbed with unsteady certainty.
I wondered what it was they knew the mountain had.

They would pass the last house, Lambert's, where
A violent gander, too old by many a Christmas,
Blared evil warning from his bitten moor.
Then it was open world, too high and clear
      For clouds even, where over heather
The free hare cleanly ran, and the summer sheep.

I knew this; and I knew all summer long
Those visionary gangs passed through our lanes,
Coming down at evening, their arms full
Of cowslips, moondaisies, whinberries, nuts,
      All fruits of the sliding seasons,
And the enormous experience of the mountain

That I who loved it did not understand.
In the summer, dust filled our winter ruts
With a level softness, and children walked
At evening through golden curtains scuffed
      From the road by their trailing feet.
They would drink tiredly at our wall, talking

Softly, leaning, their sleepy faces warm for home.
We would see them murmur slowly through our stiff
Gate, their shy heads gilded by the last sun.
One by one we would gather up the used jugs,
      The glasses. We would pour away
A little water. It would lie on the thick dust, gleaming.

Ransoms

for Edward Thomas

What the white ransoms did was to wipe away
The dry irritation of a journey half across
England. In the warm tiredness of dusk they lay
Like moonlight fallen clean onto the grass,

And I could not pass them. I wound
Down the window for them and for the still
Falling dark to come in as they would,
And then remembered that this was your hill,

Your precipitous beeches, your wild garlic.
I thought of you walking up from your house
And your heartbreaking garden, melancholy
Anger sending you into this kinder darkness,

And the shining ransoms bathing the path
With pure moonlight. I have my small despair
And would not want your sadness; your truth,
Your tragic honesty, are what I know you for.

I think of a low house upon a hill,
Its door closed now even to the hushing wind
The tall grass bends to, and all the while
The far-off salmon river without sound

Runs on below; but if this vision should
Be yours or mine I do not know. Pungent
And clean the smell of ransoms from the wood,
And I am refreshed. It was not my intent

To stop on a solitary road, the night colder,
Talking to a dead man, fifty years dead,
But as I flick the key, hear the engine purr,
Drive slowly down the hill, I'm comforted.

The white, star-shaped flowers of the wood garlic, *Allium ursinum*, are usually known as ramsons; but W. Keble Martin, in *The Concise British Flora in Colour*, calls them ransoms. They grow profusely from April to June in the beech hangers above Edward Thomas's house outside Petersfield. Obviously, in the context of the poem, ransoms means much more than the usual name.

Now the House Sleeps

Now the house sleeps among its trees,
Those charcoal scratches on the sky's
Good morning, and I walk the lane
That all night long has quietly gone
Down the cold hill, and quietly up
Until it reached that darkened top
Where the shrill light of a short day
Begins again the frozen glow

Of winter dawn. I contemplate
The wealth of day that has to wait
The recognition of my eye.
Reality is what we see,
Or what my senses all achieve;
What they believe, so I believe.
Around, the ring of hills wears light
Of morning like a steel helmet

And below them, in the brown
Cleansing of its floods, runs down
The brawling river. Now the owl,
That all night held its floating call
Over the terrified hedges, climbs
In clumsy blindness to the elm's
Black safety, there flops down,
A comfortable, daylight clown;

And little animals of night
Retire as silent as the light
To sleeping darkness. Closing the door,
I leave the white fields desert for
The loss of my descriptive eye.
The sunlit measures of the day
Are unregarded. I cut bread,
Knowing the world untenanted.

And yet, although my sight must stop
At the solid wall, a world builds up,
Feature by feature, root by root,
The soft advance of fields, daylight
Reaching west in the turn of life,
Personal, created world, half
Ignorant, half understood. And I
Complete from faulty memory

And partial complexities of sense
Those images of experience
That make approximate rivers move
Through the wrong world in which I live,
Or chart a neat uncertainty
Down major roads to Nowhere City;
But at the edge of what I know
The massed, appalling forests grow.

Through the long night the rough trucks grind
The highways, gears ripping blind,
Headlights awash on the tarmac;
All night long metallic traffic,
Racks of concrete, rams of girders,
Heavy oppression of cities
Forced by a crude growling. Yet all
Are Plato's shadows on the wall,

Noises drifting among shadows,
Shadows dying among echoes,
While clear eternities of light
Shine somewhere on the perfect world
We cannot know. My shadowed field
Lies in its flawed morning, and dirt
Falls in the slow ditches. Sunrise,
And the house wakes among its trees.

Stones

On the flat of the earth lie
Stones, their eyes turned
To earth's centre, always.
If you throw them they fly
Grudgingly, measuring your arm's
Weak curve before homing
To a place they know.

Digging, we may jostle
Stones with our thin tines
Into stumbling activity.
Small ones move most.
When we turn from them
They grumble to a still place.
It can take a month to grate

That one inch. Watch how stones
Clutter together on hills
And beaches, settling heavily
In unremarkable patterns.
A single stone can vanish
In a black night, making
Someone bury it in water.

We can polish some;
Onyx, perhaps, chalcedony,
Jasper and quartzite from
The edges of hard land.
But we do not alter them.
Once in a million years
Their stone hearts lurch.

The One Leaf

An oak leaf fell from the tree
Into my hand almost, so I kept it.
First in my fingers, very carefully,
Because it was mine. I wiped it,
Put it on my desk, near the typewriter.
Last autumn, there were oak leaves falling everywhere.

I could have chosen from so many.
It lay there months, turning browner,
Before I no longer saw it. Now
Here it is again, an old letter
From plenty. From where I stand
This is the one leaf, in the cold house, on the cold ground.

It's Somebody's Birthday

This birthday man
Rises from my hot bed
Into his mirror.
When I groan
Out of his crumpled head
He prods my dewlap with a jeering finger.

Behind his eyes
Lie the slim silver boys
Called by my name.
No blind surprise
Nor moving without noise
Shall ever startle them inside that frame.

To my round skin
He will remain flat true,
Warning for warning.
I pull my stomach in,
March a hard step or two,
Shut loud the bathroom door, murder his morning.

Drummer Evans

There was a great elm in Drummer Evans's garden.
Half of his house it kept in daylight shadow; all summer
A chaffinch sang in its highest branches, swinging
In an invisible cage its music was so local.
Drummer dribbled it crumbs from his fingers
As he sat on a log, his back to the elm trunk,
One slow leg straight before him, and his yellow hand,
His fingers, playing intricate patterns on his other knee.
He was small, his eyes looked upward always.
His face was mild and ivory, composed and smooth.
He wore a black suit and a very wide hat and he called
All women Mrs. Jones, because it was easier.
I went to him Tuesdays and Saturdays for lessons.

My kettledrum set on its three-legged stand,
He would flick its resonance with a finger and say,
"Now boy, two with each hand, away you go; and
Don't let the drumstick tamp." Tamp was a word for bounce,
We always used it. Away I'd go, two with each hand,
Back of the wrists to the skin, sticks held lightly,
And clumsily double beat with each hack fist,
Tap-tap, tap-tap, tap-tap, until that unskilled knock
Snarled in my tired arms and stuttered out.
I don't remember getting any better, but he'd nod,
Still for a while his drumming hand, and smile,
And say, "Again." When I could play no more he'd take
      the sticks
And give to my stubborn drum a pliant eloquence.
I'd leave then. The bird was nearly always singing.
It never rained in Drummer Evans's garden.

Because I knew that I would never make
On an echoing hull those perfect measures
Heard in my head as I marched at the head of armies

Or rattling between the beat of my running heels,
I left the Drummer.
                                    It was an idle sun
Recalled his garden, and an unclaimed bird
Singing from a thorn his tame bird's song
That brought the old man back,
Martial hands parading and muttering.
I went by the river's edge and stone bridge
To his thundering cottage.

For the air for half a mile was rhythmical thunder.
Roll after roll of exact, reverberant challenge,
The flames of history unfurled their names from my books,
Agincourt, Malplaquet, Waterloo, Corunna,
And I reached at a gasp the Drummer's beleaguered garden.

Ringed by standing friends at the rim of his anger,
He stood strapped for war from the fury of their kindness,
Striking his sharp refusal of all pity
The women offered. "Come on," they called, "Ah, come
        on Mr. Evans."
But he swept them away with the glory of his drumfire,
Hands flying high in volleys of retaliation.
The tree held its sunlight like a flag of honour
And helpless, uniformed men spoke out to him softly;
But his side-drum returned defiance for this old man
Whose proud skill told us he was Drummer Evans,
No common mister to be hauled to the Poorhouse.

Winter Song

Over the bluff hills
At the day's end
The diffident snow
Swirls before dropping

Blow wind, blow
That we may see
Your smooth body

The humble snow
Is waiting for darkness
So its soft light
Can muffle the hills

Blow wind, blow
The copse will be silent
The black trees empty

At the day's end
The small snow is scurrying
White bees in the moon
And the flying wind

Blow wind
Over the cold hills
For the moon is voiceless

Grass

I walk on grass more often
Than most men. Something in me
Still values wealth as a wide field
With blades locked close enough
To keep soil out of mind. It is a test
Of grass when I push a foot
Hard on its green spring. The high pastures
I mean, open to the unfenced wind,
Bitten by sheep.
     Go into Hereford,
My grandfather said (his dwarf
Grass was scarce as emeralds,
The wet peat crept brown into his happiness),
In Hereford the grass is up to your waist.
We could not gather such unthinkable richness,
We stared over the scraped hill to luscious England.

Behind us the spun brook whitened
On boulders, and rolled, a slow thread
On the eyes, to bubbling pebbles.

I have been in wet grass up to the waist,
In loaded summer, on heavy summer mornings,
And when I came away my clothes, my shoes,
My hair even, were full of hard seeds
Of abundant grass. Brushes would not remove them.

Winters, I know grass is alive
In quiet ditches, in moist, secret places
Warmed by the two-hour sun. And as the year
Turns gently for more light,
Viridian grass moves out to lie in circles,
Live wreaths for the dying winter.

Soon roots of couch-grass,
Sly, white, exploratory, will lie
Bare to my spade. Smooth and pliable,
Their sleek heads harder
And more durable than granite.
It is worth fighting against grass.

Space Miner

for Robert Morgan

His face was a map of traces where veins
Had exploded bleeding in atmospheres too
Frail to hold that life, and scar tissue
Hung soft as pads where his cheekbones shone
Under the skin when he was young.
He had worked deep seams where encrusted ore,
Too tight for his diamond drill, had ripped
Strips from his flesh. Dust from a thousand metals
Silted his lungs and softened the strength
Of his muscles. He had worked the treasuries
Of many near stars, but now he stood on the moving
Pavement reserved for cripples who had served well.
The joints of his hands were dry and useless
Under the cold gloves issued by the government.

Before they brought his sleep in a little capsule
He would look through the hospital window
At the ships of young men bursting into space.
For this to happen he had worked till his body broke.
Now they flew to the farthest worlds in the universe:
Mars, Eldorado, Mercury, Earth, Saturn.

The Dead

(after the Welsh of Gwenallt, 1899-1969)

Reaching fifty, a man has time to recognise
His ordinary humanity, the common echoes
In his own voice. And I think with compassion
Of the graves of friends who died. When I was young,

Riding the summer on a bike from the scrapyard,
Kicking Wales to victory with all I could afford –
A pig's bladder – how could I have known
That two of my friends would suffer the torn

Agony of slimy death from a rotten lung,
Red spittle letting their weakening
Living into a bucket? They were our neighbours,
Lived next door. We called them the Martyrs

Because they came from Merthyr Tydfil, that
Town of furnaces. Whenever I thought
I'd laugh, a cough ripped over the wall,
Scraping my ribs with cinders. It was all

Done at last, and I crept in to look,
Over the coffin's edge and the black
Rim of the Bible, at the dry flesh free
Of breath, too young for the cemetery.

And I protest at such death without dignity,
Death brutally invoked, death from the factory,
Immature death, blind death, death which mourning
Does not comfort, without tears. I bring

From my mind a small house huge with death.
Where heavy women cut sticks, deal with

The fires, the laborious garden, their little
Money dissolving in the hand. Terrible

Are the blasphemous wars and savageries I
Have lived through, animal cruelty
Loose like a flame through the whole world;
Yet here on Flower Sunday, in a soiled

Acre of graves, I lay down my gasping roses
And lilies pale as ice as one who knows
Nothing certain, nothing; unless it is
My own small place and people, agony and sacrifice.

Owls

The owls are flying. From hedge to hedge
Their deep-mouthed voices call the fields
Of England, stretching north and north,
To a sibilant hunt above ditches;
And small crawlers, bent in crevices, yield
Juice of their threaded veins,with

A small kernel of bones. It was earlier
I walked the lace of the sea at this south
Edge, walked froths of the fallen moon
Bare-legged in the autumn water
So cold it set my feet like stones
In its inches, and I feel on breath

And ankles the touch of the charged sea
Since. I saw in my lifting eyes the flat
Of this one country, north stretching,
And north. I saw its hills, the public light
Of its cities, and every blatant tree
Burning, with assembled autumn burning.

I know the same sun, in a turn
Of earth, will bring morning, grey
As gulls or mice to us. And I know
In my troubled night the owls fly
Over us, wings wide as England,
And their voices will never go away.

A True Death

for Vernon Watkins, 1906-1967

When summer is dead, when evening
October is dying, the pendulum
Heart falters, and the firm
Blood hangs its drops in a swing
Of stone. Laughing, we catch breath
Again. But this was the true death

Our rehearsals imitate. I lived
On the charred hills where industrial
Fires for a hundred years had grieved
All things growing. On still,
On the stillest days, a burnish
Of sea glinted at the world's edge

And died with the sun. There
Were twenty miles of Wales between
My streams and the water lore
He knew. He watched the green
Passages of the sea, how it rides
The changing, unchanging roads

Of its hollowing power. Caves
From his flooded cliffs called to him,
Dunes with their harsh grasses
Sang, the river-mouths spoke of home
In Carmarthen hills. Small stones
Rang like bells, touching his hands.

Last year we sat in his garden,
Quietly, in new wooden chairs,
Grasshoppers rasped on the hot lawn.
Shadows gathered at his shoulders
As he spoke of the little tormentil,
Tenacious flower, growing there still.

Old Voices

First the one bell, heavy, behind it
Centuries of controlled certainty, swung
With an enormous sound past
The kneeling city; it is the first
Heard stone in an architecture of ringing.
And sung in at built intervals, at
The joint of locked structure, the voice
Of the second bell. The foundation is

Set on unimpeded air. An age
Of cut stone and iron – those old
Technologies – has its immense medieval
Tongues bellowing again. Now all
The small bells filigree and stretch
A long nave in the ear and a pulled
Spire of sailing clamour. Resonant
Cathedrals of listening are launched

On the open day. But bells are not
Peaceful; are arrogant with the complete
World of their origin. Think, imagine,
In the clack of swords they began,
Short on their own shields the flat beat
Struck, so that erratic courage set
Hard in the metal; then the high edge,
Turning in the urgency of the charge,

Rang through the heads of wives
At their keen mourning. Hacking the bent
Angles of helmets, rough blades cracked again
The wombs that bore these splintered heads
In their early down. From such sounds,
From the held quiet after, the brazen
Complexities of the loud tower grew.
There was time for the patterns of victory,

And space on the fat plains of grain
For building of flawless bells. The lost
In their slate hills had tongues only,
Grew old in the slow labour
Of changing myths. Through the mist
Of altering voices their stories spun,
Through generations of telling. Spiral
Images from the belfries, the metal

Confections of chiming, are not
For the mountains. Old men tell
Of an impermanent peace, a fragile
Faith is passed through narrative
Villages in syllables of live
Whispers. Foolish now to regret
Centuries of locked exile. It happened.
We have heads full of easy legend

And elegies like the cold sun
Of treeless autumn. I carry
Such tunes in my head like the thin
Silence the bells hang in. But from
These reaching fields my surnamed
Fathers came, the great cathedrals
Counted them. I walk their lanes,
My shoes cover the concave stones

Worn by their slow tolling.
If I speak with the quick brooks
Of the permanent hills, in my saying
See hordes of the dark tribes stand,
Their faces hidden, my hand
In its perfect glove of skin holds
Other ghosts. We step the streets
Uneasily, disturbed by bells.

from MOUNTAINS POLECATS PHEASANTS

Stone and Fern

It is not that the sea-lanes
Are too long, nor that I am not
Tempted by the birds' sightless

Roads, but that I have listened
Always to the voice of the stone,
Saying: Sit still, answer, say

Who you are. And I have answered
Always with the rooted fern,
Saying: We are the dying seed.

Barn Owl

Ernie Morgan found him, a small
Fur mitten inexplicably upright,
And hissing like a treble kettle
Beneath the tree he'd fallen from.
His bright eye frightened Ernie,
Who popped a rusty bucket over him
And ran for us. We kept him
In a backyard shed, perched
On the rung of a broken deck-chair,
Its canvas faded to his down's biscuit.
Men from the pits, their own childhood
Spent waste in the crippling earth,
Held him gently, brought him mice
From the wealth of our riddled tenements,
Saw that we understood his tenderness,
His tiny body under its puffed quilt,
Then left us alone. We called him Snowy.

He was never clumsy. He flew
From the first like a skilled moth,
Sifting the air with feathers,
Floating it softly to the place he wanted.
At dusk he'd stir, preen, stand
At the window-ledge, fly. It was
A catching of the heart to see him go.
Six months we kept him, saw him
Grow beautiful in a way each thought
His own knowledge. One afternoon, home
With pretended illness, I watched him
Leave. It was daylight. He lifted slowly
Over the Hughes's roof, his cream face calm,
And never came back. I saw this;
And tell it for the first time,
Having wanted to keep his mystery.

And would not say it now, but that
This morning, walking in Slindon woods
Before the sun, I found a barn owl
Dead in the rusty bracken.
He was not clumsy in his death,
His wings folded decently to him,
His plumes, unruffled orange,
Bore flawlessly their delicate patterning.
With a stick I turned him, not
Wishing to touch his feathery stiffness.
There was neither blood nor wound on him,
But for the savaged foot a scavenger
Had ripped. I saw the sinews.
I could have skewered them out
Like a common fowl's. Moving away
I was oppressed by him, thinking
Confusedly that down the generations
Of air this death was Snowy's
Emblematic messenger, that I should know
The meaning of it, the dead barn owl.

At Usk

On a cold day, in the church-
yard, between the gate and
the west door's unlocked arch,

lay the flat stone. It was
anonymous. It might have
gained by chance its grace

of simple effigy, round
eyeless head, rough torso,
a hint of sleeping child

in its stillness; a brown
stone of Monmouthshire
shaped and polished by rain.

A child was kneeling there,
absorbed, concentrating,
measuring with happy care

on the cold of breast
and throat her offering
of snowdrop and crocus.

She matched the flowers,
placed them on the stone
child with her red fingers,

and then ran off to some
warm house in the town.
Now on the stone a film

of winter sap sticks the
limp stalks, but it is
the child at home that I

think of as I walk quickly
through God's still acre.
Her gifts delight me, and I

am leaving Usk, moving
toward the M4, clearly
right to praise the living.

A Glass Window,
In Memory of Edward Thomas,
at Eastbury Church

The road lay in moistening valleys, lanes
Awash with evening, expensive racehorses
Put to bed in pastures under the elms.
I was disappointed. Something in me turns

Urchin at so much formality, such pastoral
Harmony. I grumble for rock outcrops,
In filed, rasping country. The church drips
Gently, in perfect English, and we all

Troop in, see the lit window, smile, and look
Again; shake out wet coats. Under your name
The images of village, hill and home,
And crystal England stands against the dark.

The path cut in the pane most worries me,
Coming from nowhere, moving into nowhere.
Is it the road to the land no traveller
Tells of? I turn away, knowing it is, for me,

That sullen lane leading you out of sight,
In darkening France, the road taken.
Suddenly I feel the known world shaken
By gunfire, by glass breaking. In comes the night.

The Green Bridge

What shall we write about, in
Wales, where the concentration
Camps are a thousand years old,

And some of our own making?
I live in England, seem English,
Until my voice and wider

Eloquence betray me: then
I am a discovered alien.
I walk on Teifi banks, through

Snowdrops left us by the Romans,
Watching the river pour to death
In the sea, the February sea

Where Irish wailing thinly rides
The water. I have a blood group
Common only in Carmarthenshire.

The Wales I walk is a green bridge
To death – not yet, please God –
On which I am not lonely;

But journey on, thinking of
The dead Irish; hearing, far off,
The owners of Africa calling for freedom.

Burning the Bracken

When summer stopped, and the last
Lit cloud blazed tawny cumulus
Above the hills, it was the bracken

Answered; its still crests
Contained an autumn's burning.
Then, on an afternoon of promised

Cold, true flames ripped
The ferns. Hurrying fire, low
And pale in the sun, ran

Glittering through them. As
Night fell, the brindle
Flambeaux, full of chattering

We were too far to hear, leapt
To the children's singing.
"Fire on the mountain," we

Chanted, who went to bed warmed
By joy. But I would know that fires
Die, that the cold sky holds

Uneasily the fronds and floating
Twigs of broken soot, letting
Them fall, fall now, soft

As darkness on this white page.

Mountains Polecats Pheasants

I have seen these hills closed
By impassive winter, and stood,
Banging my arms, on the last
Cold yard of road before snow
Came down on memory, the way

Strange as Asia. In summer,
Loss of the travelled sun drops
A bulk of mountain into shadow
Deep enough to lose a town in,
And scared cars, smaller, run

For the lit valleys. I thought
The mountains safe in my mind
From all revelation, but
Had never before driven late
Their cleft passes. Midnight

Had left the road as I climbed
The foothills, the car slotted
Behind headlights and the warmed
Engine humming at gradients
Above the farms. Fenceless

The ponies slept, their fetlocks
Still, their wild skulls fallen
To stone. It was a dark
Palpable as ice on those
Stone ranges. On a blunt rise,

Where the wind scorched black
The stump hawthorns and hedge
Grass bent thick in the shock
Of wind, I saw in my lights
Such tiny brilliances. Not cats',

Not foxes' eyes shone colder.
Cutting the engine, I softened
Downroad to where they were:
Polecats, the mother stiff
With instinct, her emeralds of

Sight full on my pointing;
Her five young, caught
In a lesson of hunting.
Fear moved her, sliding her
Flat as oil and under

The light; but her innocents
Stayed, weaving their baby heads.
They mewed, their sweet throats
Tame as milk. Their gentling
Cries showed me their kindling,

Blind in a hard nest under
The piled rocks. I knew the slit
Of their eyes against the thunder
Of light. I wished for them
A lenient dark and safe home.

Last year, in true daylight,
At a faultless eighty on
Other roads, it was soft
Death I passed. A bag, burst
Cushion, cracked feathers, drift-

ing after smash, the hen
Pheasant lay. There was no
Terror in that sight. When
She was puffed to one side
In a bundle of snapped

Shafts, she lay roundly where
She fell. The slow blood
Failed to mark the air
For her, but in the fallen
Wreaths of her plumes ran

Her dozen chicks, no more
Than hours after hatching.
I could not catch them, nor
Could I harry them to safe
Hiding before rough

Death wiped their brief
Smudges under the wheels
Of cars. The stuff of
The roads, oil, grit, fine
Dust, absorbed their stain.

There was nothing to show for them,
Though they came from the perfect
Eggs this mother alone could form.
When she died, feathers hung
A week in the hedge, turning

Black in the hot exhausts.
I know that my polecats
Are old now in the deaths
Of their needed victims,
I know there are cold times.

When the fields whistle
In fear of them, the grass
Thickens as they ripple
Through, tearing murder. Yet
I would have had them meet,

Polecats and pheasants, on
Their common hills. I would
Have had them live, and
In a night more terrible
Than the terrible fall

Of shadow or winter over
These mountains I close again,
Let the truth turn clear
For them, the last whimper
Of it, true hunted, true hunter.

Beachmaster

His mother, from the loving sea
Lurching, found him by smell,
Though the nursery beach
Was thick with milk, and other
Blubber. Her comfort was all
Tacky liquid and the touch

Of nuzzle and rubbery flipper.
Weak and thin at first, he was
Afraid of water. But grew
Lusty, casting in plump sleep
His long, white, birthday fur.
In a ring it lay. He was

Left miniature sleek seal.
After three weeks she abandoned
Him, the call of heavy bull
In the sexual tide and swell
Being too much, though he moaned
With his pup's silk mouth the whole

Of a day. That night he snarled
At the spray and set off.
In ten weeks such a pup, in
Its first green diving of
The seaways, untaught, alone
In bottle-coloured water,

Swam six hundred miles, to Spain.
That was not my pup, though he
Savaged fast shoals in places
Far away, and dragged his growing
Awkwardly over other beaches.
This is his country, where young

Cows come out to call him home
And meadows of the sea swing
Miles deep under him. Here
He first fought, nostrils popping
In muscled water, in fury
Of instinct, for a territory.

He keeps ward off shore, armour
Of scar thickening shoulder
And neck; hulk bull, upright
In lull. Nobody sees him eat.
On the loud beach, his sons, small,
Weak, wait for white fur to fall.

July the Seventh

Drugged all day, the summer
Flagged in its heat, brutal
Weather sullen as brass.
There was no comfort in darkness.
Hotter than breath we lay

On beds too warm for moving,
Near open windows. Full of
Spaces the house was, walls
Fretting for a brisk air.
A door slammed flat in its

Loud frame, banging us awake.
Wind was bringing in the storm.
Quick switches of whipped light
Flicked the rooftops, made shadowless
The ends of rooms. The stopped clock

Marked the lightning. I got up
Heavily, shut the house against
Thunder. Rain was a long time
Coming, then sparse drops, stinging
Like metal, hit the bricks, the hot

Pavements. When it sweetened
To plenty, the streets tamed it,
Flowed it in pipes and conduits,
Channelled it underground through
Stony runnels. The rain brought

So faint a smell of hay I searched
My mind for it, thinking it memory.
I lay freshly awake on the cool sheets,
Hearing the storm. Somewhere, far off,
Cut grass lay in files, the hay spoiling.

In October

Moving into fall, I give my body rest
After heady summer. The hills turn early blue,
       The rivers are rising.

Yesterday, winds from the untempered north
Put me shutting windows. At night I closed my eyes
       On the last of summer.

I have set the fire, collecting the slight
Twigs. Spent as leaves, I watch my fallen hands,
       The bark hardening.

Skulls

Last night the snow came,
And again we face
Honest weather. The fence
That held its rose
So lightly is bent now
Under splintering snow.
It's winter. A flint cold
Has turned the house around

And the door hums in the wind.
If I went into the field,
Hearing the dry trees groan
In their barren cracking,
I would feel bones
Underfoot, winter's bones
Through snow, the furrow
Harder than the plough.

The ground's bone-hard. I first
Heard this in a place
Where snow was kindness.
Amazed, we had forced
Hard grass with our boots
Until it snapped. The clouds
Were scooped by easterlies
That set us hopping. It was

Our pink bones we imagined
Broken on that playground.
Long after a long snow,
After its memory,
When the sky had grown
Generously warm and sudden
Over as much world
As I remembered,

I went through a clarity
Of light in the early
Morning. And I climbed,
Climbed higher in the warmed
Hills than ever before.
Far away the sea
Burned, but I turned
To the last height

The growing sun could reach;
Then over it. Winter's touch
Lay there, unflawed
In a lake of snow
Below the peak. It was
A still depth, silence
For the raven's eye,
Holding its circled

Cold against the wreck
Of warmer seasons. Sprawled rock
Marked it, and a little
Moss. The world was all
Stillness; there was
No breathing in the place.
Skulls, the skulls of
Ponies, lay calmly dead above

The three-month snow, neckbones
Bent into snow, snow
Between the yellower hoops
Of their ribs. I had
Surprised them in their old
Deaths. Meek, vulnerable,
Stripped of flesh, muscle,
The last excuse of sinew,

They lay in a season
Too deep for sun,
For any weather to bother them.
Should the hornet
Perch in the empty
Pit of the eye, they
Would not startle. Let
Solid ice form

Its weight of the waterfall,
They would not huddle
Under the cliff. Their
Teeth, innocent of fear,
Were bare for birds to
Pick over. I let them lie,
The low dead in their cold,
While I caught at the comfort

Of breath. When I let fly
A wild call through
The hilly dark, momently
The birds eased from the
Ledges, croaked, then
Lofted home. Again
I called, but nothing moved.
A mountain silence filled

The rock crevices.
I think of those open skulls
When winter comes, and coldest
Air reveals us. I lace
Heavy boots, break brittle ice,
Feel winter's bones
Under the snow. I hold
My skull to the wind.

Elegy for David Beynon

David, we must have looked comic, sitting
there at next desks; your legs stretched
half-way down the classroom, while
my feet hung a free inch above

the floor. I remember, too, down
at The Gwynne's Field, at the side
of the little Taff, dancing with
laughing fury as you caught

effortlessly at the line-out, sliding
the ball over my head direct to
the outside-half. That was Cyril
Theophilus, who died in his quiet

so long ago that only I, perhaps,
remember he'd hold the ball one-handed
on his thin stomach as he turned
to run. Even there you were careful

to miss us with your scattering
knees as you bumped through
for yet another try. Buffeted
we were, but cheered too by our

unhurt presumption in believing
we could ever have pulled you down.
I think those children, those who died
under your arms in the crushed school,

would understand that I make this
your elegy. I know the face you had,
have walked with you enough mornings
under the fallen leaves. Theirs is

the great anonymous tragedy one word
will summarise. Aberfan, I write it
for them here, knowing we've paid to it
our shabby pence, and now it can be stored

with whatever names there are where
children end their briefest pilgrimage.
I cannot find the words for you, David. These
are too long, too many; and not enough.

A Small War

Climbing from Merthyr through the dew of August mornings
When I was a centaur-cyclist, on the skills of wheels
I'd loop past The Storey Arms, past steaming lorries
Stopped for flasks of early tea, and fall into Breconshire.
A thin road under black Fan Frynych – which keeps its
     winter
Shillings long through spring – took me to the Senni valley.

That was my plenty, to rest on the narrow saddle
Looking down on the farms, letting the simple noises
Come singly up. It was there I saw a ring-ousel
Wearing the white gash of his mountains; but every
Sparrow's feather in that valley was rare, golden,
Perfect. It was an Eden fourteen miles from home.

Evan Drew, my second cousin, lived there. A long, slow man
With a brown gaze I remember him. From a hill farm
Somewhere on the slope above Heol Senni he sent his sons,
Boys a little older than I, to the Second World War.
They rode their ponies to the station, they waved
Goodbye, they circled the spitting sky above Europe.

I would not fight for Wales, the great battle-cries
Do not arouse me. I keep short boundaries holy,
Those my eyes have recognised and my heart has known
As welcome. Nor would I fight for her language. I spend
My few pence of Welsh to amuse my friends, to comment
On the weather. They carry no thought that could be mine.

It's the small wars I understand. So now that forty
People lock their gates in Senni, keeping the water out
With frailest barriers of love and anger, I'd fight for them.
Five miles of land, enough small farms to make a heaven,
Are easily trapped on the drawing-board, a decision
Of the pen drowns all. Yes, the great towns need

The humming water, yes, I have taken my rods to other
Swimming valleys and happily fished above the vanished
Fields. I know the arguments. It is a handful of earth
I will not argue with, and the slow cattle swinging weightily
Home. When I open the taps in my English bathroom
I am surprised they do not run with Breconshire blood.

Rhydcymerau

(after the Welsh of Gwenallt, 1899-1969)

The green blades are planted to be timber for the third war,
In the earth of Esgeir-ceir and the meadows of Tir-bach,
Near Rhydcymerau.

I remember my grandmother at Esgeir-ceir,
Pleating her apron by the fire,
The skin of her face as yellow as a manuscript of Peniarth,
And the old Welsh on her lips, the Welsh of Pantycelyn.
She was part of the Puritan Wales of the last century.
I never saw my grandfather, but he was a character;
A small, quick, dancing creature –
And fond of his pint.
He had bounced straight out of the eighteenth century.
They raised nine children;
Poets, deacons, Sunday School teachers,
The natural leaders of that small community.

My uncle Dafydd, nature poet and local wit,
Used to farm Tir-bach.
His sly little song about the rooster was famous in the
farms:
  "The little cockerel is scratching
  Now here, now there, about the garden."
I spent my summer holidays with him,
Watching the sheep, and making lines of cynghanedd,
Englynion and eight-line songs in seven-eight measure.
He in turn had eight children,
The first a minister with the Calvinistic Methodists,
And also a poet.
We were a nest of poets in our family.

And now there are the trees, only the trees.
Usurping roots sucking the soil dry;
Trees, where once it was neighbourly,
An army of forest where clean pasture was,
The bastard Saxon of the south instead of poetry and
    scripture.
The dry cough of the fox has precedence
Over the voices of child and lamb.
And in the dark centre
Is the lair
Of the English Minotaur;
And on the trees
As on crosses
The bones of poets, deacons, preachers and teachers of Sunday
    School
Bleach in the sun.
And the torrent of rain washes them, they are dried by the
    rubbing wind.

Bridges

Imagine the bridge launched, its one foot
Clamped hard on bedrock, and such grace
In its growth it resembles flying, is flight
Almost. It is not chance when they speak
Of throwing a bridge; it leaves behind a track
Of its parallel rise and fall, solid
In quarried stone, in timber, in milled
Alloy under stress. A bridge is

The path of flight. A friend, a soldier,
Built a laughable wartime bridge over
Some unknown river. In featureless night
He threw from each slid bank the images
Of his crossing, working in whispers, under
Failing lamps. As they built, braced spars,
Bolted taut the great steel plugs, he hoped
His bridge would stand in brawny daylight, complete,

The two halves miraculously knit. But
It didn't. Airily they floated above
Midstream, going nowhere, separate
Beginnings of different bridges, offering
The policies of inaction, neither coming
Nor going. His rough men cursed, sloped off,
Forded quite easily a mile lower.
It was shallow enough for his Land Rover.

I have a bridge over a stream. Four
Wooden sleepers, simple, direct. After rain,
Very slippery. I rarely cross right over,
Preferring to stand, watching the grain
On running water. I like such bridges best,
River bridges on which men always stand,
In quiet places. Unless I could have that other,
A bridge launched, hovering, wondering where to land.

from *WATER VOICES*

Christmas Day

Winter drought, and a parched wind
Roughens the mud. Wrapped in a parka,
Leaning bleakly into the slack
The blast misses as it screams over

The blackthorn, I'm tramping a
Chalk ditch from the downs. Leaves
Dry as cornflakes crack under
My gumboots, the hedge is against

My shoulder. Sands of their flying
Dusts hunt the spent fields, ice
Grains stick at my eyes. Caught
On the thorns, a rip of newsprint

Shivers its yellow edges, grows
Long, then rises easily, a narrow
Heron, out of shadow. It rises,
Trailing its thin legs, into cold

Sun flat as the land. Upright,
Broad wings spread, neck curved
And head and great blade turned
Down on the lit breast, it hangs

Against barbs, against winter
Darkness, before its slow vanes
Beat once over the elms, a
Christ crucified, a flying Christ.

Lear at Fifty

This morning early, driving the lanes in my
  Glib metal, frost fur on the brambles,
The grass, the hasps and bars of gates, first
  Sun burning it away in clinging wisps,
I saw an old man, sweeping leaves together, outside
  The Black Horse. His face held night's

Stupor, the lines of his age had not stiffened
  Against the daylight. He shifted his
Feet to careful standing, and then his broom,
  His necessary crutch, moved like an
Insect on slow, frail, crawling legs from
  Leaf to leaf. The small gusts of

My passing broke his labour, heaps of the dry
  Work spilling and flying. Nobody
Walked on the shore. Waves, unexpected heavy waves
  From some wild, piling storm away at sea,
Ripped the mild sand, smashed rocks, and shot the
  Squalling gulls out of the filth, vomit

And glittering sewage the flung birds flocked for,
  And truly, the tide was high this morning;
Old shoes, cans, cynical gouts of accidental oil,
  Plastic bottles, ropes, bubbling detergent
Slime, all were thrown to the sea wall. I have
  No wish to remember those unwelcoming

Waves I turned my back on, nor to think of old men
  Sitting tight in their skulls, aghast
At what their soft, insistent mouths will keep on
  Yelling. But through the limpet hours
I've walked the fields as if on a cliff's edge,
  The idea of flight in me, and seen my

Friends, myself, all strong, governing men, turned
  Sticks, turned tottering old fools.
The last sun in its blaze brings yellow light
  To everything, walls, windows, water;
A false warmth. In the morning some old man will start
  To sweep his leaves to a neatness.

i.m. James Chuang, MB, BS, MRCS, RN

died April 23 1978, aged 25

Last Thursday morning, watching a haul of barges
tug their blunt ropes under Chelsea Bridge,
I saw two swallows, hot from Africa,
flick and scream across the delighted river.
First of the warming year, emblem and omen,
one for each day of all that remained of your life.

Jim, I can't understand how anyone as young
and generous could go so swiftly into death.
It was good that afternoon, walking in Hyde Park,
watching the little goldeneye, pair by pair
in meticulous black and white, bobbing
on the cold Serpentine. To see them dive!

They'd slip under the water so casually,
without taking breath, without preparation
slide into the silence, longer and deeper,
until we couldn't see them. They all came back.
One by one all popped up from their underworld,
out of their darkness. Small London children,

playing with grandparents, clapped their hands
at each abrupt return. We spoke of your work
at Greenwich Hospital, the Seamen's Hospital
down by the widening Thames, and I was startled
by the wholeness of your compassion, your serious
tolerance. You were a chosen man. Somewhere

away from my awareness you had come of age.
And since then I've been finding it difficult
to remember you as a small boy, that brush-head,
the apricot-coloured child who would bring his

reading book, or that older one in Christ's
Hospital blue, alert, smiling, always eager.

On Thursday afternoon I knew you the full man,
conscious of healing, able to keep death at bay
down there near the river. Images of your childhood
were not wanted. You had become my contemporary,
although you were young enough to clap your hands
with the children, and I stand in an older body.

(Conscious of certain wreck, Jim, I had meant
to ask about arthritis, how my fingers stiffen;
but had not thought to know the pain of knocking
these words out.) To think a starling's nest,
untidy tangle of instinct pressed messily
into an air vent, could have killed you.

Anger meant little to you. If I am angry
it is a futility you must allow me now.
Two Canada geese, those heavy winter birds,
grey on a grey sky, beat overhead, trailing
silence behind their ponderous flying.
A cold evening has come back to the country.

At the Sea's Edge,
in Pembrokeshire

Peter de Leia, dead eight
hundred years, began this
structure. Not having the
saint's art, nor learned
his psalter from a gold-
beaked pigeon, he built
in common stone. He exalted
labour into a stone praise.

Nor was he baptised in live
waters conveniently burst
forth to supply the shaken
drops for that ceremony. To
reach his pulpit he climbed
a joiner's steps, did not expect
the ground to lift in a sudden
hillock so that he could preach
in open piety to the rapt Welsh.

When he laid down the square-
ended presbytery, with aisles,
transepts, tower and nave, he saw
his masons bleed if the chisel
slipped. One fell in his sight
from the brittle scaffolding
and the two legs snapped
audibly, hitting the ground.
He had not the saint's skill

to stop that falling which must
fall. Such clear faith was not
possible, the rule of the world
grown strong. He knew that right

building was a moral force, that
stone can grow. An earthquake
has tested this cathedral. In
Pembrokeshire, near the saint's
river, at the edge of the sea,

de Leia built well, saw stone
vault and flower. A plain man,
building in faith where God
had touched the saint, he saw
the miracle which is not swift
visitation, nor an incredible
suspension of the commonplace,
but the church grown great about us,
as if the first stone were a seed.

Unchanging

Every seven years, is it, the body's
Changed? Flake by dry flake the skin
Renewed, glands and muscles altered
Secretly in their smooth liquids?
Hair, nails, how we shear them away,
Slow modifications unnoticed almost,
Until one day an accident of the mirror
Shows the remade man, grown different

Silently. All's changed then; eyes,
Manipulation of the senses, the very
Instruments of love are changed. The world's
Grown calcinous. What miracle, when
That which we call the heart is still
Immutable constancy, unchanged love.

Cave Paintings

i After Dark

After dark, police sirens rip us
Awake. We crouch, hands over ears, our walls
Too small to hold such raucous invasion.

In Woodland Park, in caves
Of municipal concrete, the wolf
Shivers, the cougar shakes her chained ears.

ii A Dish of Pebbles

Pebbles in a dish: opal, jade,
And one against sufficient light
A palpable smoke. All these

Are from Californian beaches. But here's
From Oregon a stone, from the castellated
Rim of the continent, its moats holding

Sea-lions, voices of moist caves. Spray
Decorates the sky, the rattle of draining
Pebbles runs south from river-mouth to river-

Mouth. Here are sharks' teeth, two, for
Needling, bloodletting. And I have arrowheads:
This, from Washington; that, of greater age, from
    Somerset.

iii A Thrush

The thrush comes into the house, I hear
Its soft battering against the window glass.

And I leave my desk, speaking to it,
Tolerate its panic, its round, wild eye,

The way it spreads its wings in a bare
Ache against the pane. I am accustomed

To creatures, release it. It leaves behind
Two slight feathers, the yellow stain of its droppings.

iv Ancestor

There is no photograph, but I think him
Tall. He stood in twenty acres of grass
And a whole unfenced mountain uprose

Behind him. Certainly he worked
Eight sons timid, ruled all daylight,
Roaring at animals. Left, at the end,

Nothing, but was the last of us, long
Ago, to come off that brutal soil with
Innocent power. So I think him tall.

v In Still Clay

A Staffordshire greyhound, fawn, couchant,
Thin, stylised neck and flexible white hocks,
He sits in still clay on a dais of royal blue.

Six inches in length, the glaze crazed
Nowhere, and one gold line untarnished
Along the hollow plinth, he is preserved

By lucky accident. Pharoahs knew his like.
He dreams in the shadow between two shelves,
Linking time with time. Is a potent hunter.

vi Scatterings of Light

Waterfalls, pools, streams, rivers,
And the loud, monotonous, empty

Drop through the centuries; the cave
Remembers water, was drilled

By water. Scatterings
Of light floated among bats

Pendulous as fruit in the rock's
Cold branches. A dry cave holds

Darkness to its walls, as water
Holds the shape of its flowing.

vii Paperweight

This domed, heavy glass, it satisfies
The hand. Its concentric flowers, whorls,

Shells and coloured rods, its airy
Bubbles even, all are held in a still

Dance. I keep it for its solid
Roundness against time, and for the men,

In France two hundred years ago, who by
Some perfect means of their mortality

Made it, full and heavy, from fragile silicas,
And sent its casual permanence to my hand.

viii Symbols

Emblems, plaques, icons, symbols
Of the decaying hand; stones, or

Feathers, identified by warm
Sight, and touched, and put

Aside; or voices,
Transferred as they vanish

In handled syllables, we keep
From the breaking dust, against

The filling of the cave. For
The cave is filling, fills

Rapidly. It closes,
From the eyes in.

Grooming

The poem stands on its firm
legs. Its claws are filed, brush
and curry-comb have worked
with the hissing groom to polish

its smooth pelt. All morning, hair
by hair, I've plucked away each small
excess; remains no trace of
barbering, and all feels natural.

It is conditioned to walk, turn
to the frailest leash, swing
without effort into ecstatic
hunting. Now I am cleaning

the teeth in its lion jaws
with an old brush. I'll set it
wild on the running street, aimed
at the hamstring, the soft throat.

The beautiful young Devon Shorthorn Bull,
Sexton Hyades 33rd

In warm meadows this bull
Ripens gently. He is a pod
Of milky seed, not ready yet.
Not liking to be alone, he
Drifts on neat feet to be near
His herd, is sad at gates
When one is taken from him. There's
No red in his eye, he does not
Know he's strong, but mildly

Pushes down hedges, can carry
A fence unnoticed on his broad
Skull. His flat back measures
The horizon. Get a ladder, look
Over him. Dream that, one by one,
The far fields fill with his children, his soft daughters.

Eagle and Hummingbird

Demure water, soft summer water,
Its rolling boulders dropped, its carried logs
Cast white as salt upon some resting beach,
I throw my spinners here, those small, beaked suns
Turning through steelheads, cut-throat, and the
Five-pound salmon come from the sea too young
Along the green channel of their instinct.

I stand midstream on rock, its roots in water,
Using the air to fly my singing line,
The burning spindle drifting through the river,
The river alders burning in the sun;
United elements, the one forgiving world
In whose veined heart I stand in a blue morning
Beneath the flash of hummingbirds, the smoulder

Of fishing eagles. Water and sun, fire
And reflected fire, the hundred suns
The river's mirror carries under the trees,
Buoyancy of the light birds, all's here,
All, all is here. And my thin line holds now
The lure of the hummingbird, its spinning
Breast, and the hooked voice of the eagle.

Ravenna Bridge

Thinking he walked on air, he
Thrust each step, stretched straight
His ankle. We saw him lift
On thinnest stone between him-
self and earth, and then dip on.

Such undulant progress! Stern
Herons walk like that; but he
Just rose again into his
Highest possible smiling air,
Stepped seriously by us,

And kept for all himself
The edges, even, of his happiness.
Passing, we caught the recognition
Of his transfiguring sweet
Smoke. And so he stepped, he

Skipped, the thin boy, on narrow
Ravenna Bridge, itself a height
Over pines and sycamores. He
Danced above their heads. If
He'd hopped the handrail, had

Swayed into flight, fallen
To stony death among wood-doves,
We should have watched him. I did
Not stand as I felt, hand
To mouth in a still gasp, but

Coldly and relaxed, and saw the boy
Perform his happy legs across
Ravenna Bridge and up the hill
To Fifty-Second. We walked home,
Thanking his god, and ours.

A Reading in Seattle

Cold snow covers the summer
Mountains; they do not reject it.
Seas towed from Asia, immense
Pacific waters, invade the bays,
Roll heavy the long coast, turn
With a shake of the spray
And splinter the bleached
Lumber, sieve the lion-
Coloured sand. Inland, with
Lakes and the tamed
Salt of the Sound, is the lovely
City, safe in its washed air,
Holding its bridges calmly,
Its trees and tended grass,
The welcome of its wooden
Houses. At night, many
Lamps glitter cleanly, form
Stars in reflecting water
By skittering winds disturbed,
By small boats softly home
From fishing. The people sleep
In a ring of Japanese hills.
A hundred miles away a cone-
Shaped mountain measures the light.

Rivers, the rivers too.
Drop by plain drop they fall
From the cracking glaciers,
Collect in forming channels,
Roar, released, torrent of jade,
Opalescent fluid jewel,
Route of the salmon's instinct.
I stood once at the Skagit's edge
On a hot day, my face burned,

And walked slowly in, one step,
And another step, until I was
Waist deep in green flowing,
One with it, with the water.
Driving away through the little
Homesteads I was bereft. No man
Stands twice in the same river.

In the evening I thought
Of Dylan, how he had read
In Seattle. "The little slob,"
My friend said, marvelling,
"He read Eliot so beautifully,
Jesus, I cried." I did not answer.
In the city now the bars are
Empty of his stories
And only the downtown Indians
Are drunk as his memory.

I read in a hall full
Of friends, students, serious
Listeners. The great dead
Had spoken there, Auden,
Roethke, Watkins, many others.
There was room for a plump ghost.
I thought I heard his voice
Everywhere, after twenty years
Of famous death. The party over,
I walked home, saw on peaks
The coldest snow, white as bone.

Belonging

He came after the reading, when all
Had left, the students, the kind
Congratulating friends, and I was tired.

What it was gave me more than a
Public courtesy for this old man,
Small, neat in his blue suit, someone's

Grandfather, I can't say. He held
A paper faded as his eyes; his family
Tree. Anxious, erect, expecting my

Approval, he stood in the hot room.
"I'm Welsh," he said. I read his
Pedigree. Bentley, Lawrence, Faulkner,

Graydon, no Welsh names. I nodded,
Gave back his folded pride, shook
My head in serious admiration. Belonging,

After all, is mostly matter of belief.
"I should have known you anywhere," I said,
"For a Welshman." He put away his chart,

Shook hands, walked into the foreign light.
I watched him go. Outside, the sprinklers,
Waving their spraying rainbows, kept America green.

Travelling West

March ends, and the wild month
Batters its last hours against the house.
Such driven rain, such a wind
Bellowing out of the west
Against the walls!
I sit in the late room,
Watch the curtains shiver, and think
Of the drenched counties of England,
Their shuddering pastures, the creaking fibres
Of oak and hanging beech.

The gutters are full, the uneasy road's
Awash; dazed cars buffet the flood
Behind their swimming headlights.
Perhaps the grey sea from the west
Has broken in at last, bringing
Its ancient flotsam, news
From the drowned islands, voices,
Branches of legendary trees.
But that old, distant coast
Will hold, it will hold always.

Although I saw it when the year
Had barely turned from summer,
The sea was snarling early,
Spun me as I swam, thrashed me
Among its grains with its upper hand,
Sank me in little storms.
Fighting for land, gasping,
Reeling, beaten deaf, I saw
The small farms in the hills
Light up their steady lamps.

Flew west over a sea spotted
With cloud, and three days later
Swam in kindlier water,
In Branch Lake, by the Penobscot River.
Had gone for togue and landlocked salmon,
But the sun lulled my hooks. I hung
In a hammock of water, warm silt soft
To the toes. Mallard
Feathered above my comfort, the long
Westering light streamed through the red oaks.

I have walked hard Pacific beaches,
Skin burned raw by an insidious sun,
Stared through high arcs of spray
At seas running with tuna and oyster shell;
A man at the world's edge, facing westward,
Aware that every tide is for departures;
And came home, a small Odysseus,
Having, as best I could, followed the sun.
I sit alert in the still room, hearing
The storm, knowing no end to the journey.

The chalk downs hold these rains
Like a sponge, releasing them
Through the villages in clear bournes.
Salad cresses grow there, and tiny fish,
Their world a yard of shallow pool,
Flicker among the thready roots.
The flood will be absorbed and turned
To mild uses. Five hours will bring
The sun up. We'll begin once more,
Travelling west, travelling west!

NEW POEMS

Berries

For the first time this year, berries
light up the garden. Stumbling downstairs,

grumbling, stubbing my sight against
a darkness I'm not ready for, I reach

for a switch, pause. In the garden
berries are incandescent. Frost

has uncovered the branches. Ignited fruit,
cotoneaster, holly, plump heps of damask,

of rosa rugosa, of the dry old noisette
nailed to the cold wall, all are blazing.

I stare in my dim awareness of autumn
passing, imagine how all over England

these sparks are lighting the winter;
round crab, the seeds of spindle

and wayfarer, clusters of buttery haw,
the waxy barberry, the black lamps

of ivy, beads of neglected briar,
of alder buckthorn, succulent

candles of yew. Perched on a chair,
I relish berries, warmed by their fatness.

Earth

Hail rattles the garden.
It scatters like white shot and
    The stung earth winces.

In summer I longed for
A cold wind. Now my neck aches
    At the first of winter.

Too late, too late!
The apple-blossom is blown and
    The sweet fruit gathered.

Like fish-scales the shine
On village roofs. The house prepares
    To reject winter.

As the leaves fall, so
The clouds multiply; it's all
    Balance, equilibrium.

Flints in the turned field,
The city's gutters, all things cry
    Endure, endure!

Dust in June, the field's
Stiff clay now; its puddles mirror
    The sullen weather.

When I was younger
I ignored dust; now I move near it,
    I watch it with love.

Is that the nestling
Which was featherless in May?
    He's hard-eyed now.

This morning the children
Raced to school. Who are these dotards
    Filling the schoolyard?

    "Consider this leaf,
Old now, dry as an egg-shell;
    It was born last April."

    As I grow older
I begin to feel how strong
    The pull of gravity.

    Turning in heaven
The pied earth; its cities move
    Into daylight, darkness.

Seven Poems from the Welsh of Dafydd ap Gwilym

The Fox – Y Llwynog

Yesterday, while I waited
For my girl in the wildwood,
Confident she would come by
(In her time she's made me cry)
I saw in the trees' green gap
Not the heartbeat of my hope,
But the curse of our kennel,
A sly fox, red animal,
Sitting there on his haunches
As tame as a tortoise.

I aimed. since I had it by,
My new bow, yew and costly,
Intending with the use of arms
To set off a few alarms,
To aim from the hill's brow
A fast accurate arrow.
Too eager, I missed. Instead
Shot the wild shaft past his head;
And to make me more angry,
Broke my bow against a tree.

Then my fury at that fox,
That marauder of meek ducks,
That harrier of fat hens,
That glutton of goose-pens!
How he hates the horn's clear call
And the hounds on his trail!
His voice is not musical,
He glows against the gravel.
Ape-faced he flits the furrows,
Stalking a stupid goose,

Scaring crows at the hills's rim,
Acre-leaper, red as flame,
Observed by the birds' high eyes,
A dragon from old stories,
A tumult among feathers,
A red pelt, a torch of furs,
Traveller in earth's hollow,
Red glow at a closed window,
A copper box with quick tread,
Bloody pincers in his head.

Don't think to follow him where
Deep in Hell he has his lair.
Russet racer, scarlet dart,
He's too cunning to be caught.
Gorse-leaper, all graceful,
Leopard, lightning in his tail.

The Thrush Singing – Y Ceiliog Bronfraith

Strong was the art and onrush
Of a flecked singer, the thrush
Who from the tree's height sprang
His unfettered singing.
Listen, oh let your ear fill!
No voice for the sorrowful,
But loud for the proud boy
And girl in early May
He whistles out a love-note
With every pulse of his throat.

Brook-clear, carol-call, day-bright,
Music lucid as light
He sang again and again,
Of happiness without pain,
Yesterday, all yesterday,
While I beneath a birch lay.

His reverend feathers on,
He reads the morning lesson
Exultant from his thicket:
He sets morning alight.
Hill-seer, light's interpreter,
Love's poet of leafy summer,
He sings as his privilege
Every song of the stream's edge,
Every soft, honey sonnet,
Every organ throb below it,
Spendthrift of his nature's art
To capture a girl's heart.
He preaches, bidding us come
To Ovid's flawless kingdom,
This bird, perfect priest of
May, headlong voice of love.

Lovers meet at his birch-tree
And he offers them freely
The deep wealth of his passion.
Or he'll sing where he's hidden
In a tangle of hazel –
Cloister-trees and bird-angel –
Songs lost by Heaven's fallen,
Songs he makes from love alone.

The Spear – Y Gwayw

I saw her there, her fair hair
Pale as foam, as white water,
From head to toe perfection,
More radiant than day-dawn.
She watched the play of Noah
In the saint's church at Bangor.
World's wonder and non pareil,
Pure flower and my betrayal,
Just to see her is for me
Greatest gift; and agony.

I'm stabbed with a seven-edged spear,
Each edge a complaint to her
That I lie pale with poison,
The gift of the men of Môn
Their envy is in my heart
And no man can pull it out.
No smith tempered this weapon,
No hand fine-ground its iron;
Without shape, without shadow,
A bitter barb brought its blow,
Subdued my splendour. I am ill
With love for Gwynedd's candle.
The long spear has pierced me,
My one thought is her beauty.
You may witness my weakness,
A sad boy with a white face,
Wearing her wounds in his heart,
Her painful skewer, her sharp dart.
She placed it there. I am killed
By a girl gold as Esyllt.

I'll wear her spear for an age,
Carry it in my rib's cage,
Endure the ache of the awl
Until death's dismissal.

The Seagull – Yr Wylan

Smooth gull on the sea's lagoon,
White as snow or the white moon,
Sun shard, gauntlet of the sea,
Untroubled is your beauty.
Bouyant you ride the rough tide,
A swift, proud, fish-eating bird.
Come to me, anchored on land,
Sea-lily, come to my hand.
White-robed, whiter than paper,
You're a sea-nun, sleek and pure.

Wide praise is for you and her;
Circle that castle tower,
Search till you see her, seagull,
Bright as Eigr on that wall.
Take all my pleading to her,
Tell her my life I offer.
Tell her, should she be alone –
Gently with that gentle one –
If she will not take me, I,
Losing her, must surely die.

I completely worship her.
Friends, no man ever loved more –
Taliesin's nor Merlin's eye
Saw a woman as lovely.
Copper-curled, curved as Venus,
How beautiful the girl is.
O seagull, but see her face,
Loveliest on the world's surface,
Then bring me her sweet greeting,
Or my certain death you bring.

The Girls of Llanbadarn – Merched Llanbadarn

Plague take them, every female!
With longing I'm bent double,
Yet not one of them, not one,
Is kind to my condition.
Golden girl, wise wife, harsh witch,
All reject my patronage.

What's their mischief, what malice
Makes them turn on me like this?
That one, with the fine eyebrows,
Can't she meet me in the trees?
There's no blame, no shame on her
To greet me in my green lair.

I have always been someone
So prodigal of passion
Not a single day goes by
But one or two catch my eye;
But here they all think of me
As some kind of enemy.
Every Sunday in Llanbadarn
There I'd be (no need to warn)
Bemused by some girl's beauty
(But my back to God's bounty)
And when I had ogled all,
Sweet-faced in seat or stall,
I'd hear one of them whisper
To the wise friend beside her:

    "See that pale boy over there,
With his sister's long hair –
Don't trust him. Look at his eyes,
They're sly and lascivious."

"Is he like that? Then no chance,"
Says the friend, with a cold glance.
"He'll not get me, you may depend.
Let him roast till the world's end!"

What payment for my passion –
I've been sent to perdition.
I have to learn to restrain
My long pleasure in love's pain,
Must pack my bundles and flit,
A solitary hermit,
Must walk the world's cold boulder,
My head over my shoulder.
To look backwards, that's my fate,
A twisted neck, and no mate.

To Jesus Christ

Immortal Jesus, spirit – of God's spirit.
    We know your pain was great;
    Sharp stab of sword, then stretched straight
    On the wooden cross, for man's merit.

Of your begetting the world knows – born
    Of a virginal girl, God's called lass.
And at your birth, Lord, the clear stars – they sang
    So early of you, *Dom'ne, Dom'nus,*
That three kings left their palaces – proud men
    Travelling humbly to your low house,
Bringing their bountiful messages – bright gold
    For You and your Mother, myrrh, frankincense.
True Father, Son of Grace – and Holy Spirit,
    Shining Lord, the one Prince of our Peace,
Was it not arrogance – I ask sadly,
    That sold our Trinity, our hope of miracles?
O treacherous Judas – O crude folly
    To turn You to your enemies,
To animal torture, pitiless – brute blows,
    Your white limbs torn, thorns biting God's face.
And the voice of justice – a beggar-judge,
    A sycophant, pilate, son of beggars.
Now come the naked flatterers – thieves,
    The sweet deceivers, a throng of Jews.
Now nine step out with ropes – brought to bind you,
    For your sacred sake, to the pine cross.
So cruel the cut of cords, the knots – now Mary
    Cries a great call above her falling tears.
Even so the end was gracious – despite the Cross
    The cold grave could not keep you, Matthew says.
When we see it for ourselves – blest Passion,
    Why is it we don't think of your groans?
Your nailed feet fill (sad memories) – with blood,

Aching for me, O God, your pierced hands;
On your beautiful head, the marks – of death,
　　Your lips turn pale, your wounds leak from spears.
And for these sad injuries – God's ordeal,
　　A hundred should attest your holiness.
From your harsh miseries – were we not blest,
　　Suffering God, when you came to us?
After your death, for us – there is no evil;
　　For Joseph too your life was welcome, Jesus.

Verses for the Mass – Englynion Yr Offeren

Anima Christi, sanctifica me.
      Merciful, famous heart of Three – and One,
         The prophets' whole glory,
        Sweet soul of Christ from the tree,
        Polish me like a jewel, cleanse me.

Corpus Christi, salva me.
      Christ's stricken body, battered – without cause,
         Communion's found bread,
        Find me not among the dead,
        With your life keep mine protected.

Sanguis Christi, inebria me.
      Christ's blood, lest for wildness – I am sent
         Into the wilderness,
        Then rise, light of God's praise,
        And keep me from drunkenness.

Aqua lateris, Christi, lava me.
      Waters of Christ's wide scars – His sore side,
         Bravely he bore the Cross –
        In those eternal waters
        Let me wash, count me no loss.

Passio Christi, comforta me.
      Christ, heaven's passion, leader – lord of prophets,
         Your five wounds were bitter;
        But strong is the power of prayer,
        Strengthen me, uphold me, Sir.

O bone Iesu, exaudi me.
      Compassionate Jesus, turn to me – a speck;
         Turn, Light of the new day;
        Lord of all worship, hear me,
        Listen, do not condemn me.

Et ne permittas me separari a te.
> Place me, my whole self, my soul – rich increase,
>> Near your hand, world's weal;
> Like a strong hedge, I'll serve well,
> Praise without pause my voice tell.

Ut cum angelis tuis laudem te.
> With a holy throng, Lord, your strong host – angels,
>> Light that will not be lost,
> You call from heaven's high post
> That we shall be saved and blest.

Amen.
> Let us come to that true kingdom – heaven,
>> In obedience come;
> Land of high grace, eternal welcome,
> Land of our faith's feasting, home.